The Breathtaking Poetry of Kim Jong Un

100% Unauthorised

Copyright 2022

Contents

I Hate America - Page 7

Doing As They're Told - Page 9

I Miss My DonnyWonny - Page 11

The Greatest of All Time - Page 13

Lies - Page 15

My Friend Den - Page 17

Brotherly Love - Page 19

Prison Camps Are Handy - Page 21

Not My Uncle Joe - Page 23

My Dad is Everywhere - Page 25

I Know Kidnappers - Page 27

No Christmas For Me - Page 29

Introduction

Kim Jong Un is more than just the leader of North Korea. He is a man with a heart and soul, and he often wears them on his sleeve.

For the first time ever in this book, Kim's love of poetry has been thrust into the mainstream.

You might imagine he sits around all day planning the next rocket test or having sex with concubines, but that couldn't be further from the truth.

When he's not busy making important decisions that affect every citizen in the DPRK, Kim loves nothing more than to sit in a scenic location with his notepad and write beautiful poems.

The world can sometimes seem like an ugly place, but with this collection of limericks and poems, Kim hopes to bring joy and spread understanding.

That said, failure to give praise for the poems in this book WILL result in execution.

Enjoy.

I Hate America

I hate America
America is bad
They tried to kill my grandfather
They tried to kill my dad
They say mean things about me
I think it's really rude
But once I get this fusion right
America is screwed!

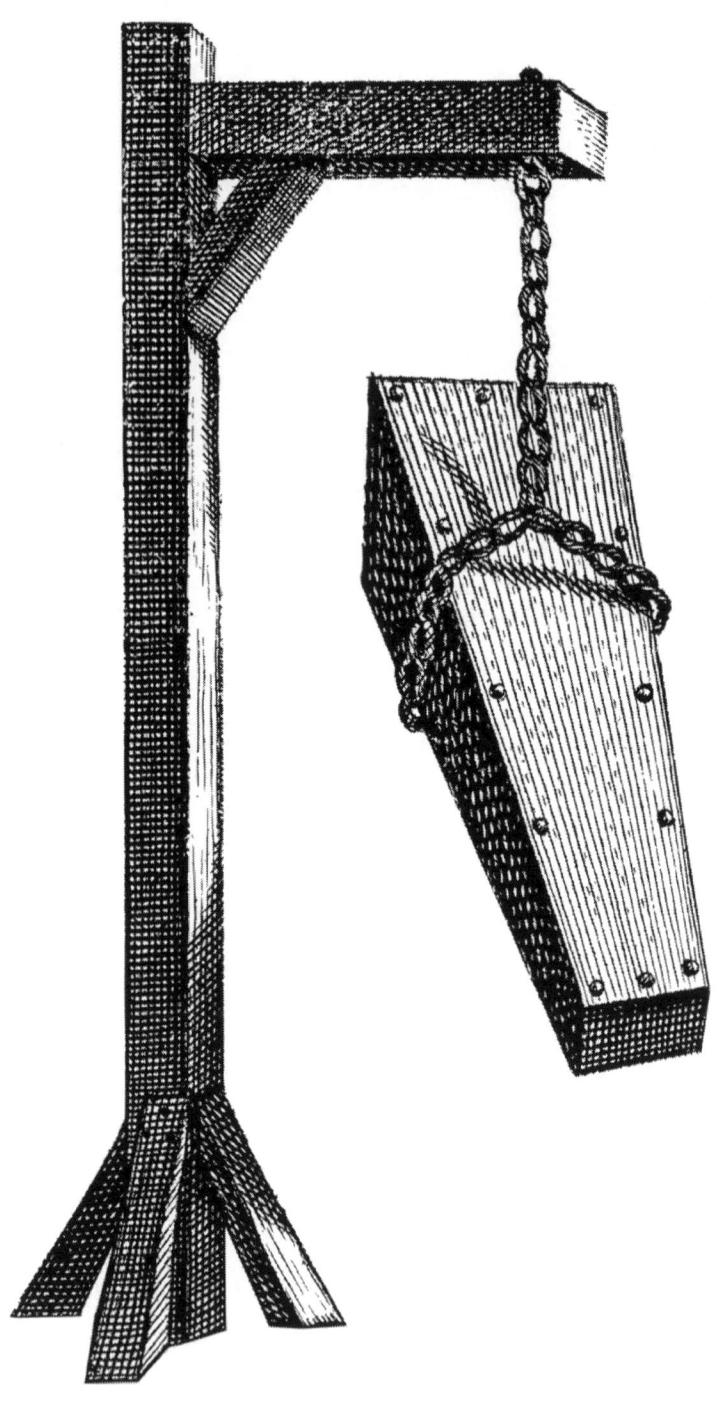

Doing As They're Told

There was a young man from Pyongyang
Who didn't sing when others sang
He soon changes his ways
As soon as I explained
If he didn't sing he'd be hanged

I Miss My DonnyWonny

Did you feel the same as me when we met
On that summer's day as you stepped off the jet?
Nobody noticed my trousers expand
As you walked over and you held my hand
Life's just not the same now, I cry every day
Donald my darling, please come back to stay

The Greatest of All Time

Mao, Stalin, Castro
Mugabi, Gaddafi, Pot
Il Sung, Jong Il, Me

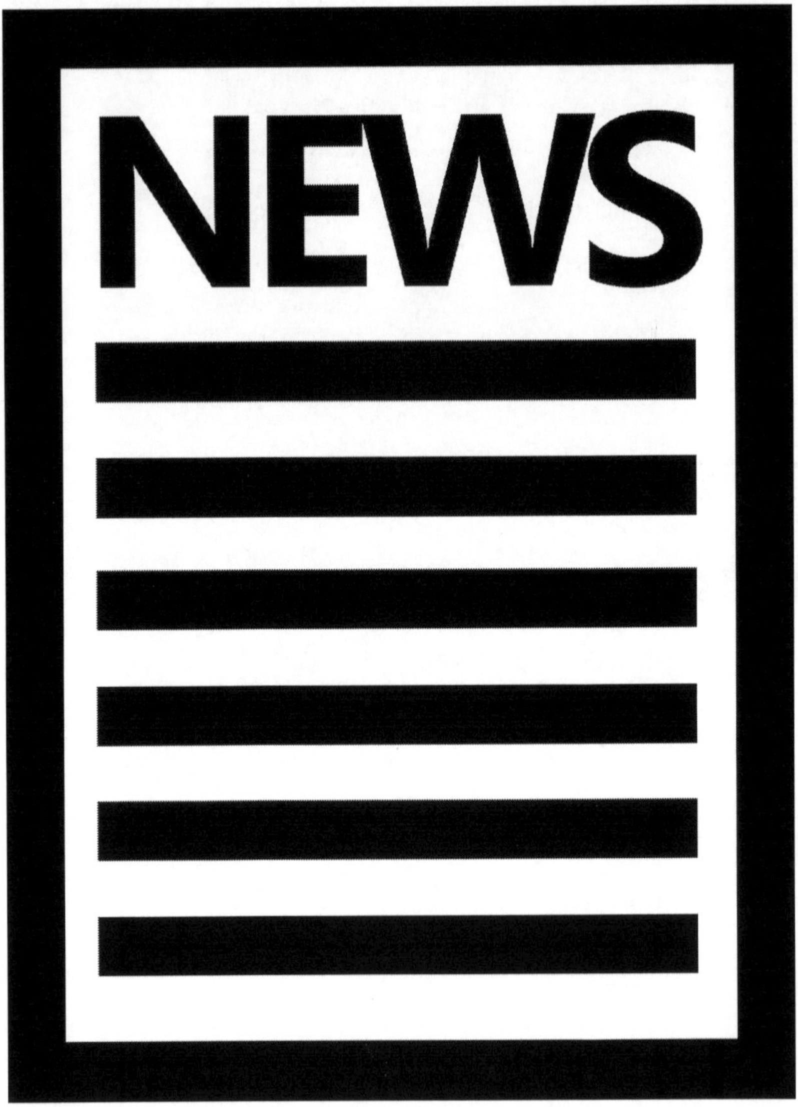
NEWS

Lies

Lies, lies, lies
That's all they ever say
They lied about me yesterday
They lied again today
They say I want to start a war
But that just is not true
They say I ride on unicorns
And that I do not poo
They like to call me "Rocket Man"
But that seems unhinged
Cuz my favourite song by Elton John
Is Candle in the Wind

My Friend Den

Basketball is good
Dennis Rodman is my friend
I will spare him, alone

Brotherly Love

My sister is the best
We laugh and joke each day
She always knows just how to cheer me up
And what to say
She listens to my problems
And she gives the best advice
She reads to be at bedtime
Before she turns out the light
My sister is the best
But I still have to say
I'll have her executed
If she tries to take my place

Prison Camps Are Handy

There once was a man on a mission
He tried to spread Capitalism
But I knew his game
So I had him framed
And threw his whole family in prison

Not My Uncle Joe

Joe Biden doesn't like me
He says we can't be friends
He never puts a single kiss
On birthday cards he sends
He doesn't want a selfie
And he doesn't want to chill
When we go out to restaurants
He never pays the bill
Joe Biden doesn't like me
It makes me feel quite sad
But in the end, we never miss
The friends we never had

My Dad Is Everywhere

I miss my dad
I miss him like mad
I miss the smile on his face
But when I feel down
I just go downtown
Cuz there's portraits all over the place

I Know Kidnappers

There was a girl from South Korea
Whose family wanted to see her
So I set a trap
And had her kidnapped
And now she is forced to live here

No Christmas For Me

Why can't I celebrate Christmas
Why can't I put up a tree
Why can't the peasants buy presents
Why can't they give them to me
Why can't I just build a snowman
Why can't I play on my sled
Why can't I forget the Day of the Sun
And celebrate Christmas instead?

Afterword

Please remember to write amazing reviews of this book and the poems contained within in.

Your life depends on it!

Printed in Great Britain
by Amazon